This journal belongs to:

All Things Bright
& Beautiful

All Things Bright & Beautiful

A Devotional Journal for Nature Lovers

Jennifer Flanders

PRESCOTT PUBLISHING
Tyler, Texas

Copyright ©2014 by Jennifer Flanders. www.flandersfamily.info

The vast majority of clip art in this book is from a set of 9 CDs my husband bought me back in 1996 called *Masterclips 101,000 Premium Images Collection*. This was long before I started blogging or writing or publishing *anything*, and I hadn't the foggiest idea what I'd ever do with such a thing — but I held onto it, just in case, and now I use it all the time!

Additional clip art from The Graphics Fairy, http://members/thegraphicsfairy.com/

ISBN: 978-1-938945-14-4
LCCN: 2015945680

Dedication

In loving admiration of
all the nature lovers in my life

Contents

Introduction

As a child, I was a bit of a tomboy. No hairbows and fancy dresses for me. I was perfectly content in my little Buster Brown short sets, climbing trees or wading through muddy creekbeds or flopped on my belly in the soft black dirt of my grandmother's garden, hunting frogs, lizards, turtles, and horned toads.

I have such fond memories of feeding ducks and catching crawdads and gathering bouquets of wildflowers. There is so much wonder to be found in God's creation, if we can manage to slow down and open our eyes to appreciate it all.

And that is what this book is really about — encouraging you to observe and explore, to record your thoughts and impressions of all you see in the natural world around you, and also to make connections between the physical and the spiritual.

There's no right or wrong way to use this journal. You can write in it, draw in it, paste pictures or mementos into it — you are only limited by your own imagination. I hope you'll have fun learning about the flora and fauna in your neck of the woods and will enjoy having a pretty place to record what you learn, to review later!

May Christ's richest blessings be yours,

Jennifer Flanders

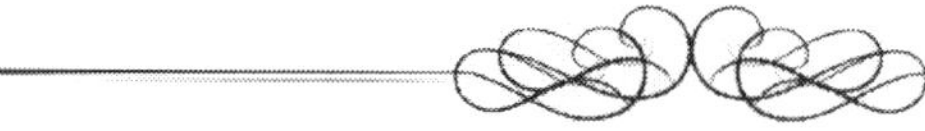

"For from Him and through Him and to Him are all things.
To Him be the glory forever. Amen."

- Romans 11:36, NASB

All Things Bright & Beautiful
by Cecil F. Alexander

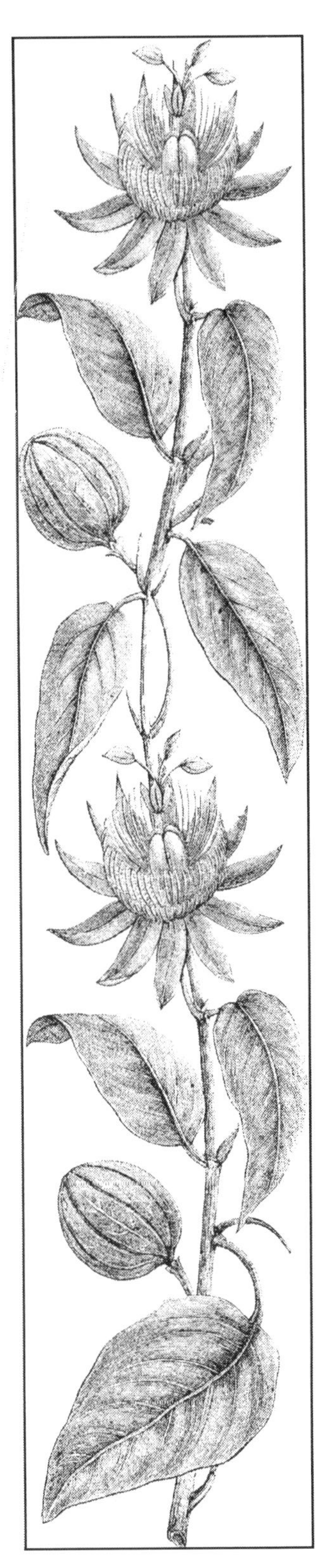

All things bright and beautiful,
All creatures great and small,
All things wise and wonderful:
The Lord God made them all.

Each little flower that opens,
Each little bird that sings,
He made their glowing colors,
He made their tiny wings.

The purple headed mountains,
The river running by,
The sunset and the morning
That brightens up the sky.

The cold wind in the winter,
The pleasant summer sun,
The ripe fruits in the garden,
He made them every one.

The tall trees in the greenwood,
The meadows where we play,
The rushes by the water,
To gather every day.

He gave us eyes to see them,
And lips that we might tell
How great is God Almighty,
Who has made all things well.

"We know that the whole creation has been groaning
as in the pains of childbirth right up to the present time."

- Romans 8:22, NIV

In the Beginning

In the beginning, God
created the heavens
and the earth...

Genesis 1:1-2

On day ONE, God
made light when
there was none.

Genesis 1:3-5

On day TWO, God
made skies and
oceans blue.

Genesis 1:6-8

On day THREE,
God made land and
plants and trees.

Genesis 1:9-13

On day FOUR, God made sun, moon, and stars galore. 

Genesis 1:14-19

On day FIVE, God made birds and fish alive. 

Genesis 1:20-23

On day SIX, God made animals & man to finish this. 

Genesis 1:24-31

On day SEVEN, God then rested in his heaven. 7

Genesis 2:1-3

"For as high as the heavens are above the earth,
so great is his love for those who fear him…"

-Psalm 103:11

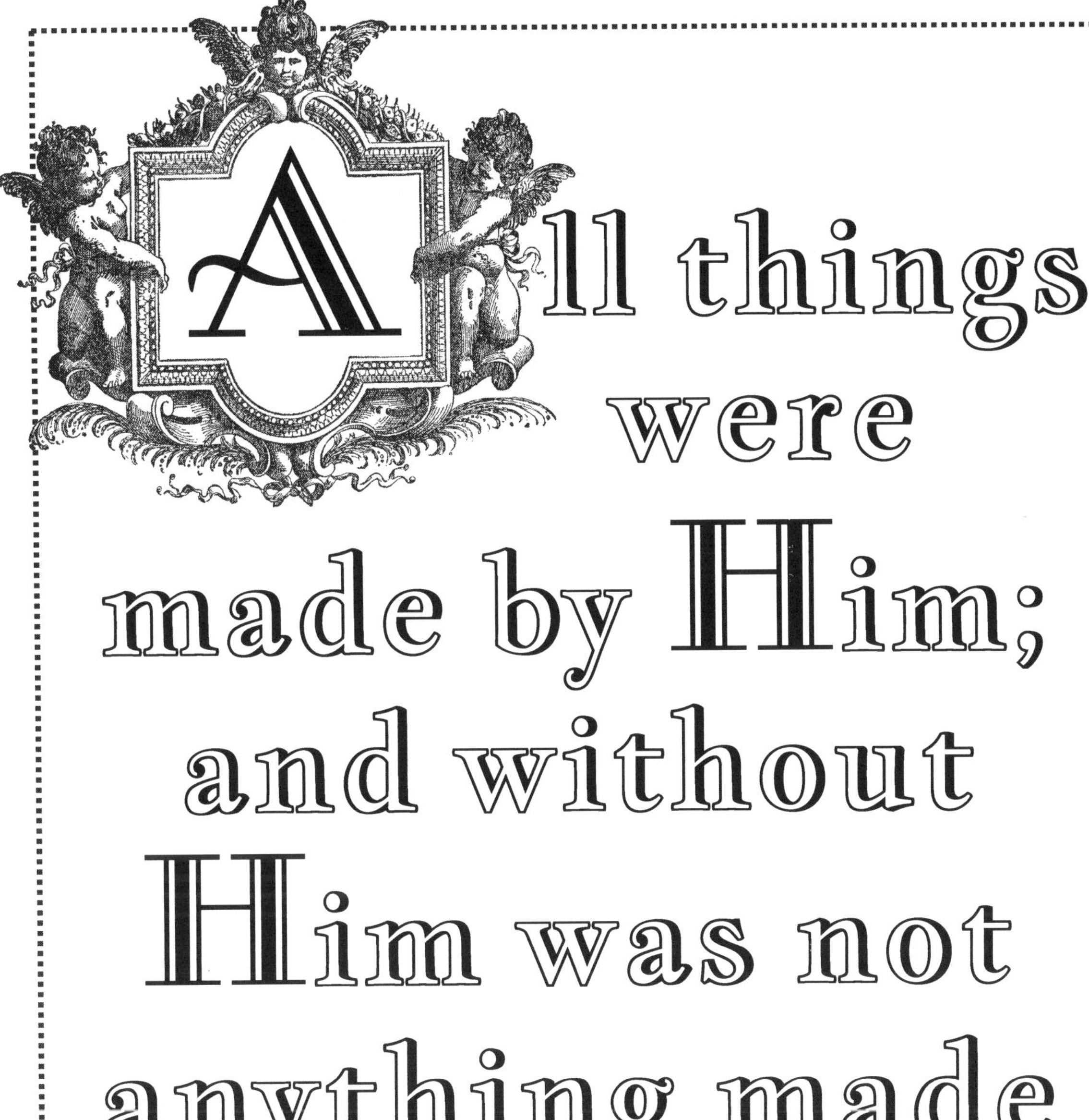

All things were made by Him; and without Him was not anything made that was made.

- John 1:3, KJV -

Am I following the Good Shepherd?

"My sheep listen to my voice; I know them, and they follow me."

- John 10:27, NIV

What the Bible says about sheep:

What does subduing the earth look like?

"And God blessed them. And God said to them,
'Be fruitful and multiply and fill the earth and subdue it...'"

- Genesis 1:28, ESV

What does it mean to have dominion?

"...and have dominion over the fish of the sea and over the birds of the heavens and over every living thing that moves on the earth."

- Genesis 1:28, ESV

Drawing Domesticated Animals:

Now Put It Into Practice:

Hidden beneath His Wing:

"...how often I have longed to gather
your children together,
as a hen gathers her chicks
under her wings..."

- Luke 13:34, NIV

Nothing in all creation is hidden from God's sight. Everything is uncovered and laid Bare before the eyes of him to Whom we must give account.

- Hebrews 4:13, NIV -

"Be sure you know the condition of your flocks,
give careful attention to your herds."

- Proverbs 27:23, NIV

Flora
& Fauna

"For behold, the winter is past, the rain is over and gone. The flowers have already appeared in the land."

- Song of Solomon 2:11-12, NASB

Consider the lilies...

"Why are you worried about clothing?
Observe how the lilies of the field grow; they do not toil nor do they spin,
yet I say to you that not even Solomon in all his glory
clothed himself like one of these.."

- Matthew 6:28-29, NASB

Be Respectful of Nature:

"If you come across a bird's nest beside the road,
either in a tree or on the ground, and the mother is sitting on the young
or on the eggs, do not take the mother with the young."

- Deuteronomy 22:6, NIV

What happens when a bird strays from its nest?

"A person who strays from home
is like a bird that strays from its nest."

- Proverbs 27:8, NLT

What does it mean to be sly as a fox?

"Catch the foxes for us, The little foxes that are ruining the vineyards,
While our vineyards are in blossom."

- Song of Solomon 2:15, NASB

Is it ever okay to outfox someone?

"Foxes have dens and birds have nests,
but the Son of Man has no place to lay his head."

- Matthew 8:20, NIV

Be innocent as doves

"I want you to be wise in what is good and innocent in what is evil."

- Romans 16:19, NASB

Oh, that I
had the wings
of a dove!
I would fly away
and be at rest.
- Psalm 55:6 -

As for you, be fruitful & multiply...

Populate the earth & abundantly multiply in it.

(Genesis 9:7, NASB)

Animals I've seen in my own backyard...

"And God made the beast of the earth after its kind, and the cattle after their kind, and every thing that creepeth upon the ground after its kind; and God saw that it was good."

-Genesis 1:25

… and what they were doing.

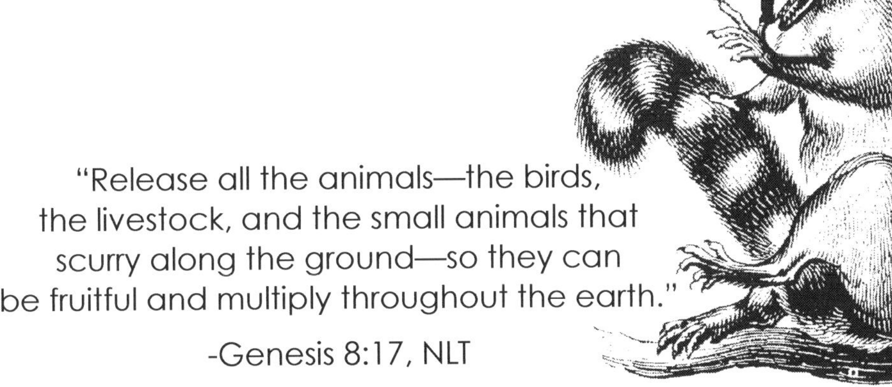

"Release all the animals—the birds,
the livestock, and the small animals that
scurry along the ground—so they can
be fruitful and multiply throughout the earth."

-Genesis 8:17, NLT

Recognizing Animal Tracks:

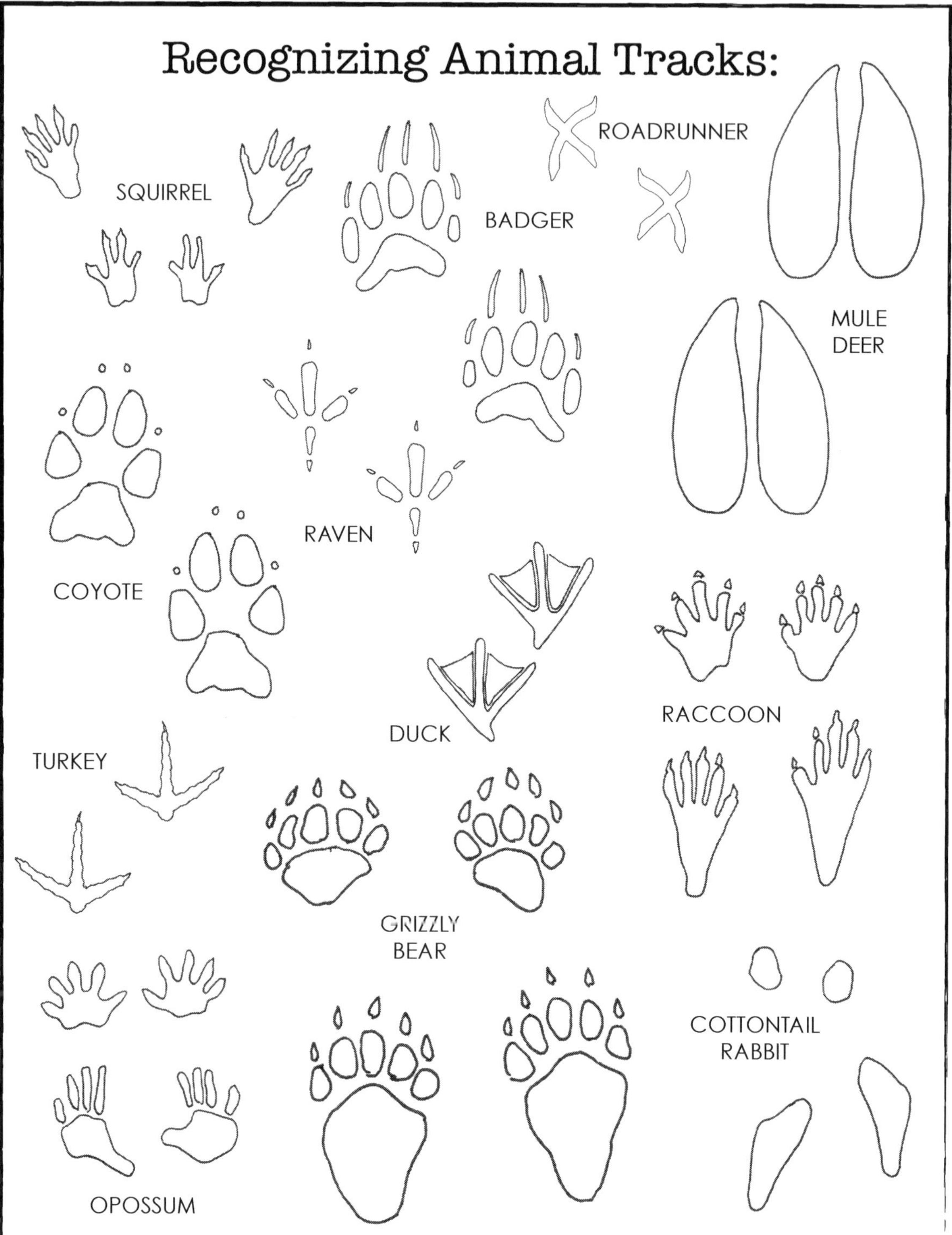

Tracks I've seen:

"My feet have followed in His tracks;
I have kept to His way and not turned aside."

- Job 23:11, HCSB

"Then will the lame leap like a deer, and the mute tongue shout for joy. Water will gush forth in the wilderness and streams in the desert."

- Isaiah 35:6, NIV

Satisfaction

"They will neither hunger nor thirst,
nor will the desert heat or the sun beat down on them."

- Isaiah 49:10, NASB

"The earth is the LORD's, and everything in it,
the world, and all who live in it."

- Psalm 24:1, NIV

Bird
Watching

"God created... every winged bird after its kind;
and God saw that it was good."

- Genesis 1:21, NASB

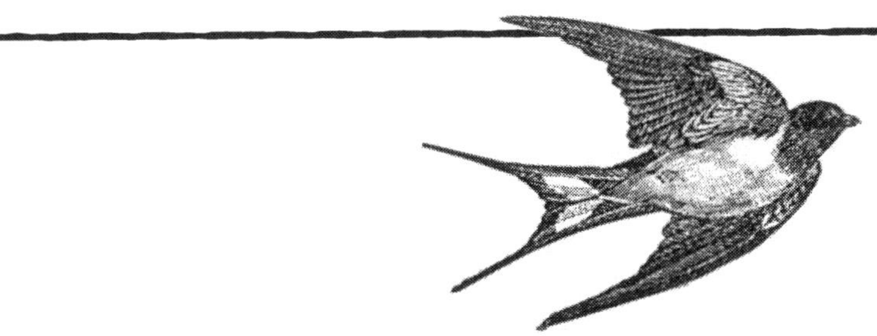

"Like a sparrow in its flitting, like a swallow in its flying,
So a curse without cause does not alight."

- Proverbs 26:2, NASB

Yet they that wait upon the LORD shall renew their strength; They shall mount up with wings as eagles, They shall run & not grow weary, They shall walk and not faint.

Isaiah 40:31

An example of how God has encircled & protected me:

"He encircled him, He cared for him, He guarded him as the pupil of His eye. Like an eagle that stirs up its nest, that hovers over its young, He spread His wings and caught them, He carried them on His pinions."

- Deuteronomy 32:10-11, NASB

Close Calls:

"Our soul has escaped as a bird out of the snare of the trapper; The snare is broken and we have escaped."

- Psalm 124:7

Birds of a feather
flock together

"Let us consider how to stimulate one another to love and good deeds,
not forsaking our own assembling together, as is the habit of some,
but encouraging one another;
and all the more as you see the day drawing near."

- Hebrews 10:24-25

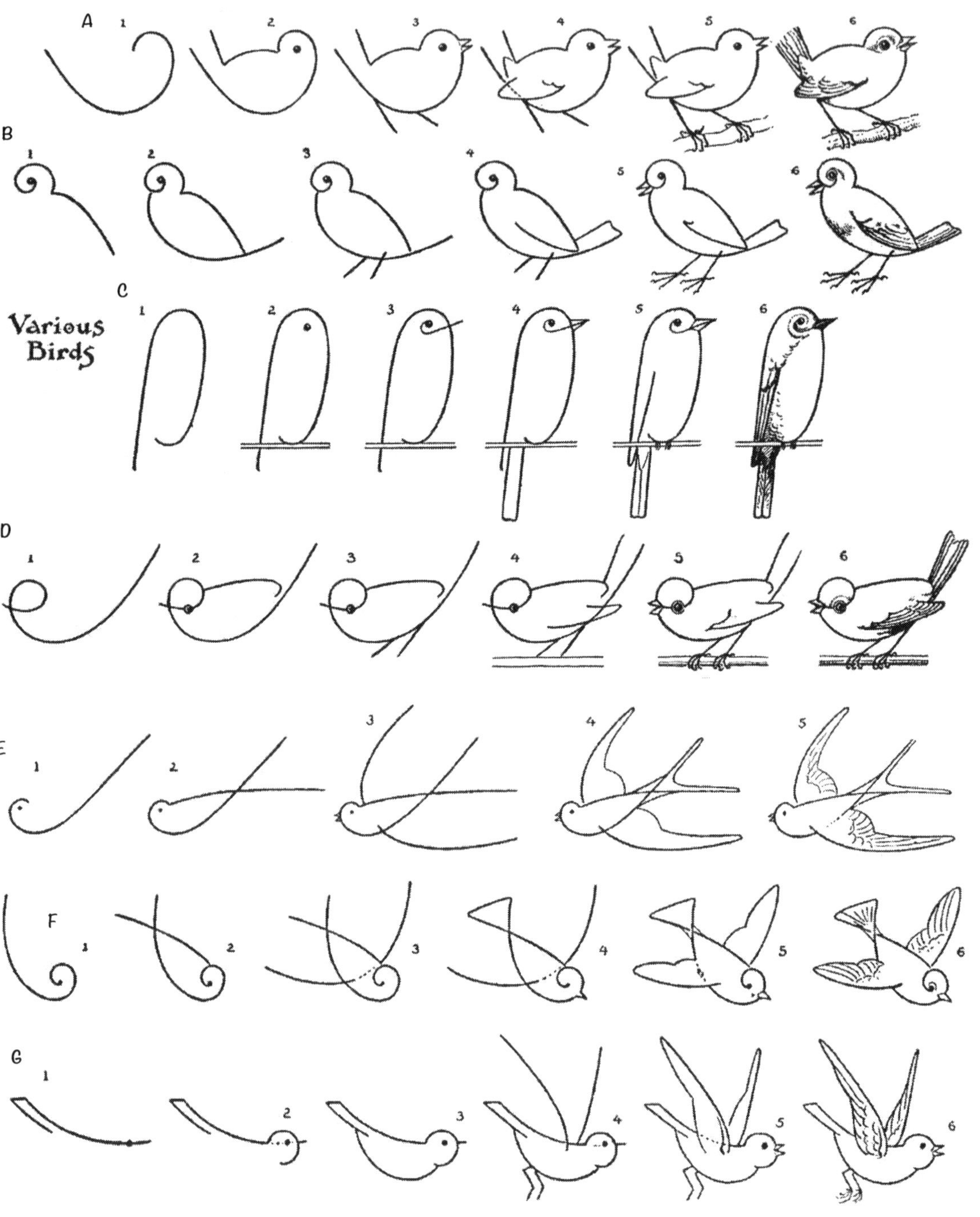

A
B
Various Birds
C
D
E
F
G

Practice makes perfect...

I must be watchful

"Stay alert, stand firm in the faith, show courage, be strong."

- 1 Corinthians 16:13, NET

THEREFORE KEEP WATCH; BECAUSE YOU DO NOT KNOW ON WHAT DAY YOUR LORD WILL COME.
- Matthew 24:42 -

"People can never predict when hard times might come. Like fish
in a net or birds in a trap, people are caught by sudden tragedy."

- Ecclesiastes 9:12, NLT

"Just as birds hover over a nest,
so the LORD who commands armies will protect Jerusalem.
He will protect and deliver it; as he passes over he will rescue it. ."

- Isaiah 31:5, NET

Peacemakers make peace.

"Now may the Lord of peace himself give you peace at all times
and in every way. The Lord be with all of you."

- 2 Thessalonians 3:16, NIV

Don't count your chickens
before they hatch.

"You do not know what your life will be like tomorrow. You are just a vapor that appears for a little while and then vanishes away. Instead, you ought to say, 'If the Lord wills, we will live and also do this or that.'"

- James 4:14-15, NASB

"Are not two sparrows sold for a penny?
Yet not one of them will fall to the ground
outside your Father's care."

- Matthew 10:29, NIV

"Look at the birds of the air;
they do not sow or reap or store away in barns,
and yet your heavenly Father feeds them.
Are you not much more valuable than they?"

- Matthew 6:26, NIV

"There the birds make their nests;
the stork has its home in the junipers."

- Psalm 104:17, NIV

"The owl will nest there and lay eggs, she will hatch them,
and care for her young under the shadow of her wings."

- Isaiah 34:15, NIV

"But I will sing of your strength,
in the morning I will sing of your love..."

- Psalm 59:16, NASB

The early bird gets the worm.

"In the morning, LORD, you hear my voice;
in the morning I lay my requests before you
and wait expectantly."

- Psalm 5:3, NIV

"He will cover you with his feathers, and under his wings
you will find refuge; his faithfulness will be your shield and rampart."

- Psalm 91:4, NIV

Wildlife

"The fastest runner doesn't always win the race,
and the strongest warrior doesn't always win the battle."

- Ecclesiastes 9:11, NLT

Fix your eyes on the prize!

"Do you not know that in a race
all the runners run, but only one gets the prize?
Run in such a way as to get the prize."

- 1 Corinthians 9:24, NIV

Full of Grace and Truth:

"Let your speech always be gracious, seasoned with salt,
so that you may know how you ought to answer each person."

- Colossians 4:6, ESV

Ugly duckling... or beautiful swan?

"For I am confident of this very thing, that He who
began a good work in you will perfect it until the day of Christ Jesus."

- Philippians 1:6, NASB

Things aren't always as they seem...

"Beware of the false prophets,
who come to you in sheep's clothing,
but inwardly are ravenous wolves."

- Matthew 7:15, NASB

… and things won't always be as they are now.

"The cow and the bear shall graze;
their young shall lie down together;
and the lion shall eat straw like the ox."

- Isaiah 11:7, ESV

My Thoughts on Cages:

Born Free:

"It was for freedom that Christ set us free; therefore keep standing firm and do not be subject again to a yoke of slavery."

- Galatians 5:1, NASB

What the Bible says about wildlife:

He watches over us all.

"I know every bird of the mountains,
And everything that moves in the field is Mine."

- Psalm 50:11, NASB

As the eer pants

for the water brooks,

o my soul

pants for You,

O od.

- Psalm 42:1, NASB

"The Sovereign LORD is my strength;
he makes my feet like the feet of a deer,
he enables me to tread on the heights."

- Habakkuk 3:19, NIV

Has a coon ever crashed your camping trip?

"The mountains offer it their best food, where all the wild animals play."

- Job 40:20, NLT

How about a bear?

"Better to meet a bear robbed of her cubs than a fool bent on folly."

- Proverbs 17:12, NIV

Drawing Woodland Creatures:

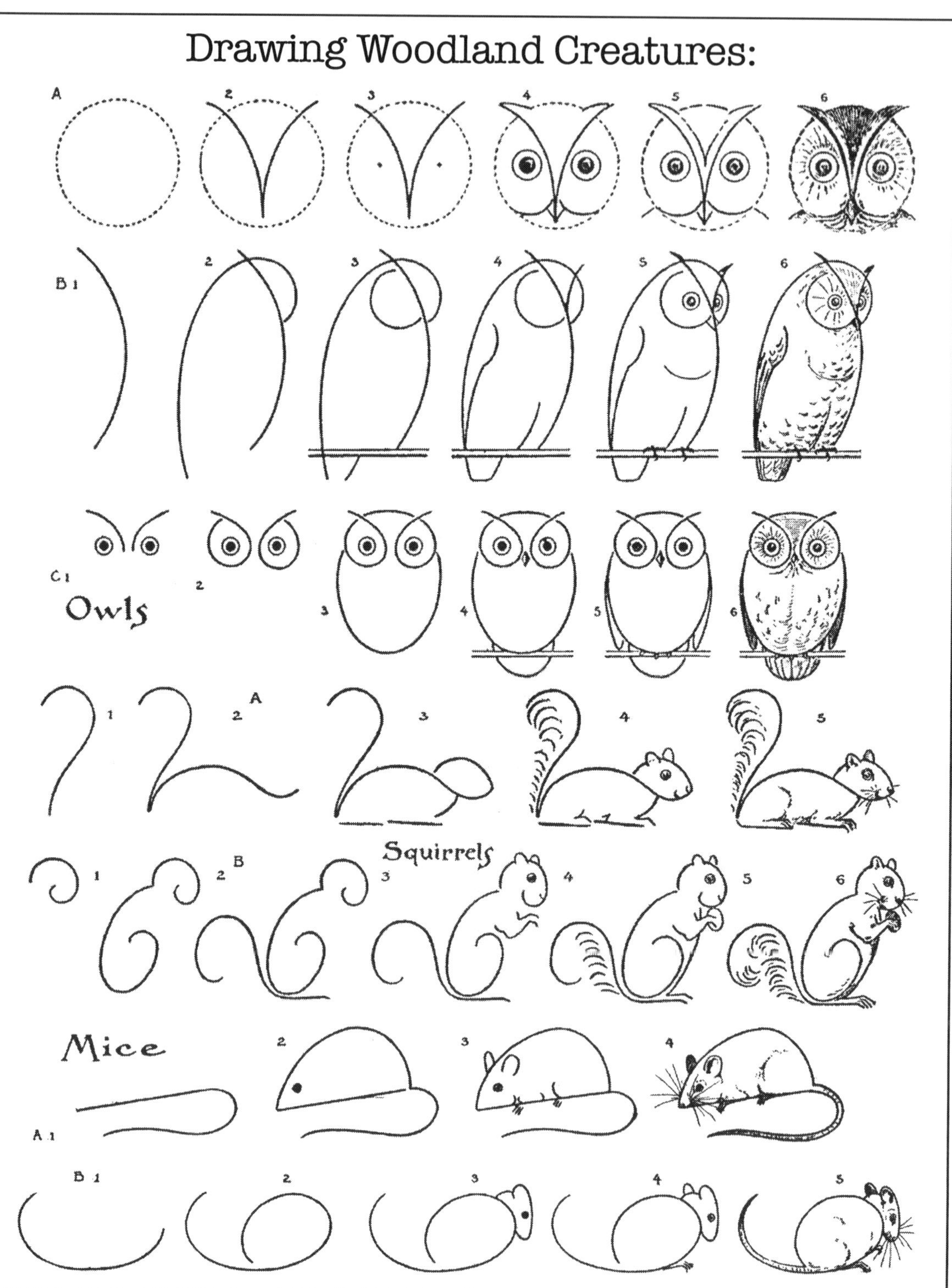

Sketch a woodland scene.

Things God gave me for my protection:

"But let all who take refuge in you be glad;
let them ever sing for joy.
Spread your protection over them,
that those who love your name
may rejoice in you."

- Psalm 5:11, NIV

How I should respond to temptation:

"Now flee from youthful lusts and
pursue righteousness, faith, love and peace,
with those who call on the Lord from a pure heart."

2 Timothy 2:22, NASB

"The rock badgers aren't a strong species either,
yet they build their dens in the rocks."

- Proverbs 30:26, ISV

Wildflowers

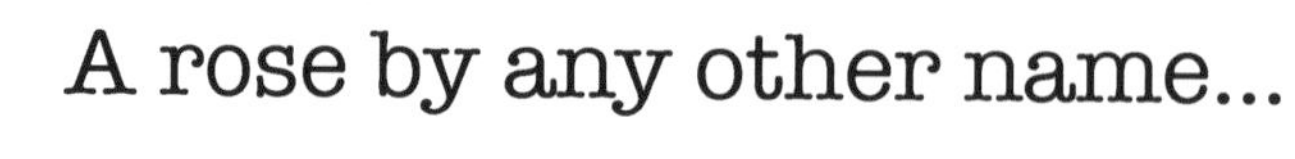

A rose by any other name...

"I am the rose of Sharon, the lily of the valleys."

- Song of Solomon 2:1, NASB

...smells as sweet.

"The fig tree forms its early fruit;
the blossoming vines spread their fragrance."

- Song of Solomon 2:13, NIV

Life is fragile...

"But the rich should take pride
in their humiliation--since they will
pass away like a wild flower."

- James 1:10, NIV

... handle with prayer.

"He will respond to the prayer of the destitute;
He will not despise their plea."

- Psalm 102:7, NIV

Favorite
Flowers

Places to
Pick Them

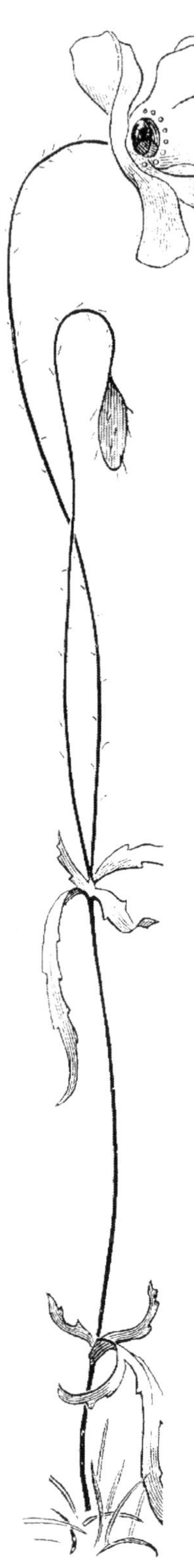

For every action...

For as the earth bringeth forth her bud, and as the garden
causeth the things that are sown in it to spring forth;
so the Lord GOD will cause righteousness and praise
to spring forth before all the nations.

- Isaiah 61:11, KJV

… there's a reaction.

"As he was scattering the seed, some fell along the path,
and the birds came and ate it up."

- James 1:10, NIV

My Life is a Fragrance

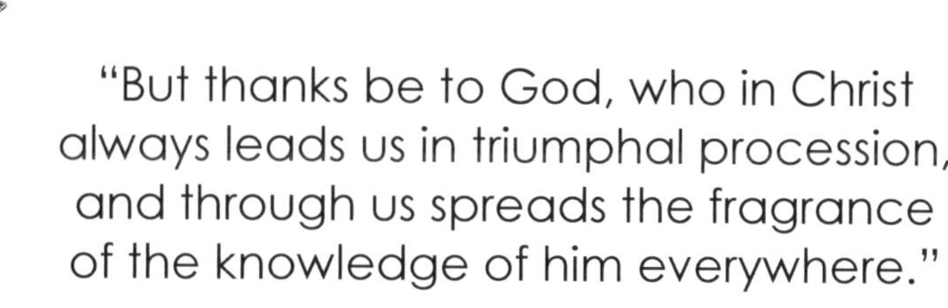

"But thanks be to God, who in Christ
always leads us in triumphal procession,
and through us spreads the fragrance
of the knowledge of him everywhere."

- 2 Corinthians 2:14, ESV

The grass withers, and the flower fades, but the word of our GOD stands forever.

— Isaiah 40:8, NASB —

Christ is my nourishment.

"Taste and see that the LORD is good;
blessed is the one who takes refuge in him."

- Psalm 38:4, NIV

I must abide in the Vine.

"Remain in me, as I also remain in you.
No branch can bear fruit by itself; it must remain in the vine.
Neither can you bear fruit unless you remain in me."

- John 15:4, NIV

A Poem about Flowers

Picking Posies:

"He is like a bouquet
of sweet henna blossoms
from the vineyards of En-gedi."

- Song of Solomon 1:14, NLT

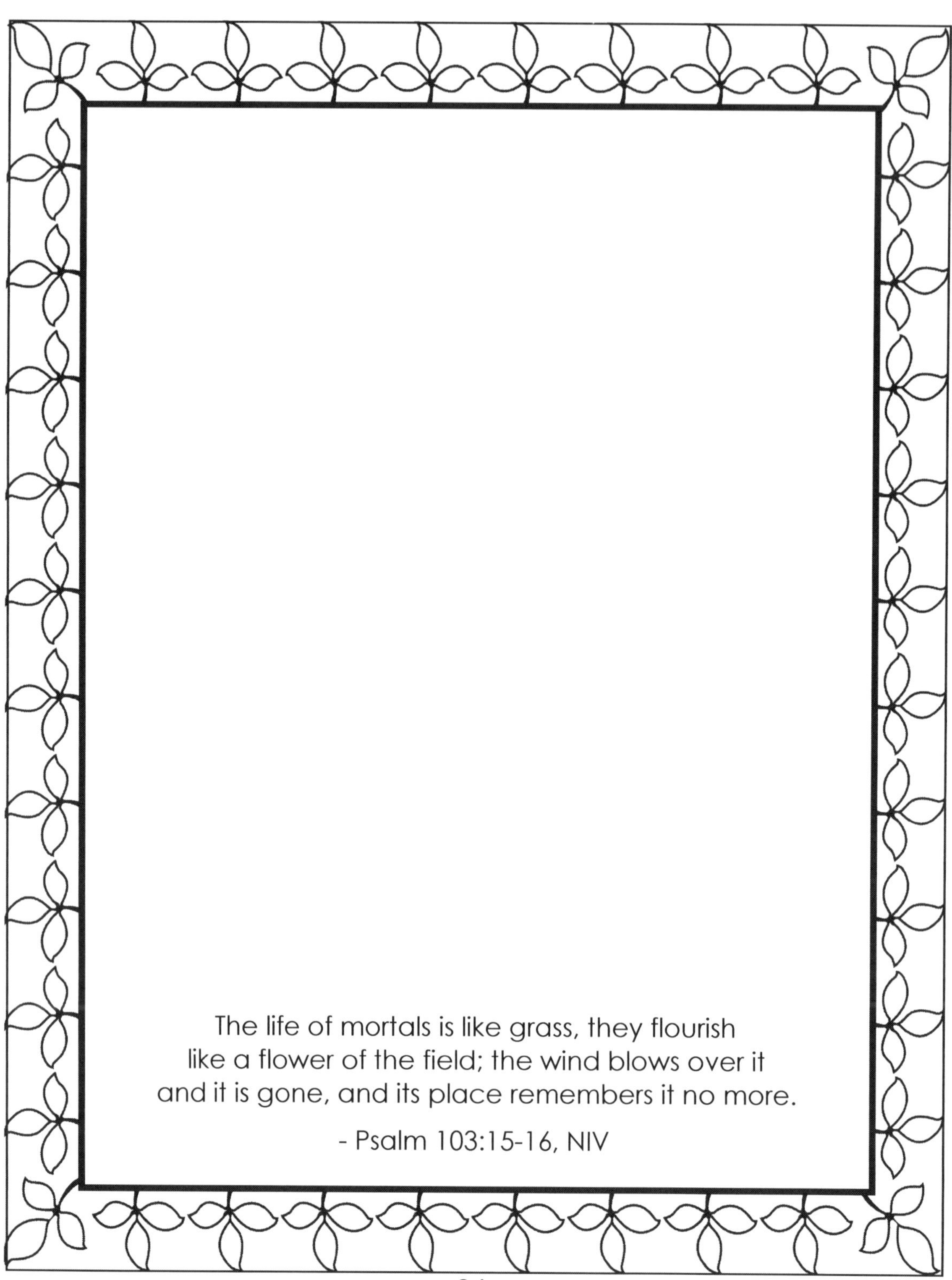

The life of mortals is like grass, they flourish
like a flower of the field; the wind blows over it
and it is gone, and its place remembers it no more.

- Psalm 103:15-16, NIV

Creepy Crawlies

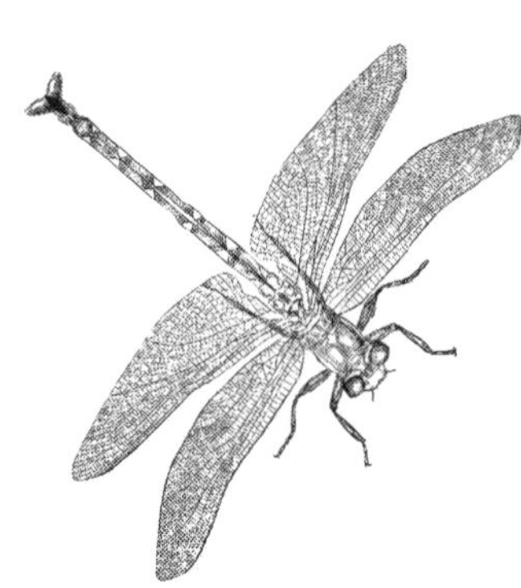

Gossamer Wings:

"When the creatures moved, I heard the sound of their wings,
like the roar of rushing waters, like the voice of the Almighty,
like the tumult of an army."

- Ezekiel 1:24, NIV

Intricate Design:

"How great are your works, O LORD!
Your plans are very intricate!"

- Psalm 92:5, NET

"The locusts came up over all the land of Egypt and settled in all the territory of Egypt; they were very numerous. There had never been so many locusts, nor would there be so many again."

- Exodus 10:14, NASB

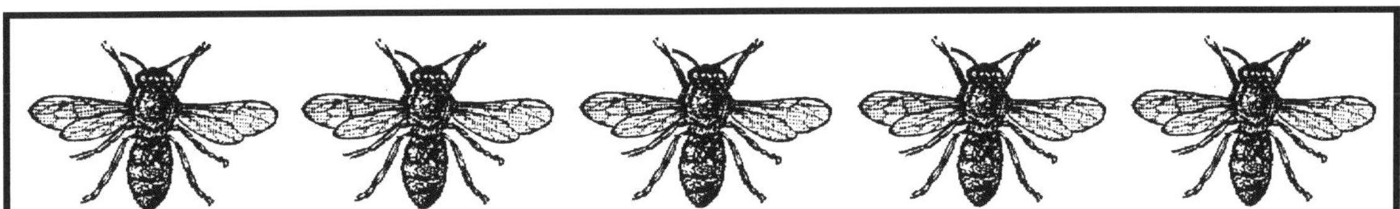

"He brought us to this place and gave us this land,
a land flowing with milk and honey."

- Deuteronomy 26:9, NIV

New Life in Christ

Ezekiel
36:26

Romans
6:4

Ephesians
4:22-24

Colossians
3:9-10

THEREFORE if anyone is in CHRIST, he is a new creation; old things have passed away, behold all things are become new.

Some things need to change...

"If you really change your ways and your actions
and deal with each other justly... then I will let you live in this place,
in the land I gave your ancestors for ever and ever."

- Jeremiah 7:5 ,7, NIV

... and others don't.

"Every good and perfect gift is from above,
coming down from the Father of the heavenly lights,
who does not change like shifting shadows."

- James 1:17, NIV

Sometimes I feel like crawling in a hole:

"When the LORD rises to shake the earth, his enemies will crawl into holes in the ground. They will hide in caves in the rocks from the terror of the LORD and the glory of his majesty."

- Isaiah 2:19, NLT

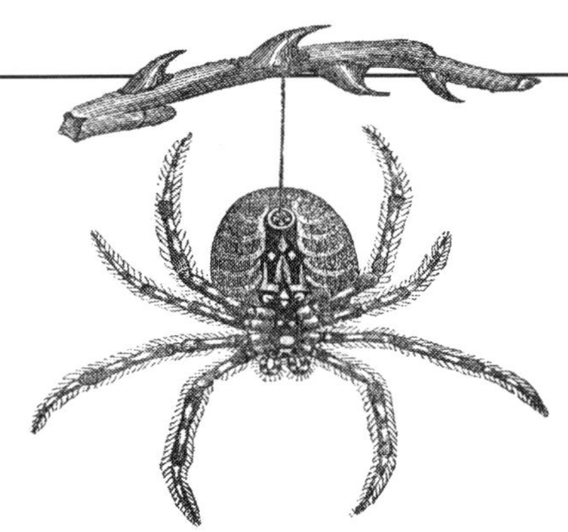

My thoughts on spiders:

"Such is the destiny of all who forget God;
so perishes the hope of the godless. What they trust in is fragile;
what they rely on is a spider's web."

- Job 8:13-14, NIV

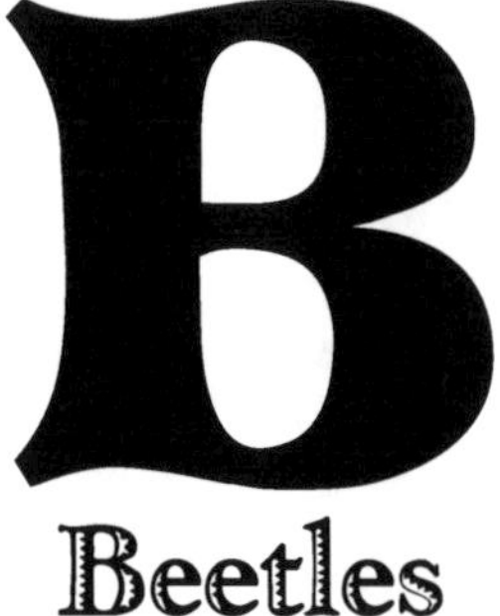

B
Beetles

U
under rocks

G go crawling

S slowly about.

"How sweet are Your words to my taste!
Yes, sweeter than honey to my mouth!."

- Psalm 119:103, NASB

The judgments of the Lord are true & Righteous altogether. More to be Desired are they than gold, yea, than Much fine gold: Sweeter also than honey and the honeycomb.

Psalm
19:9-10

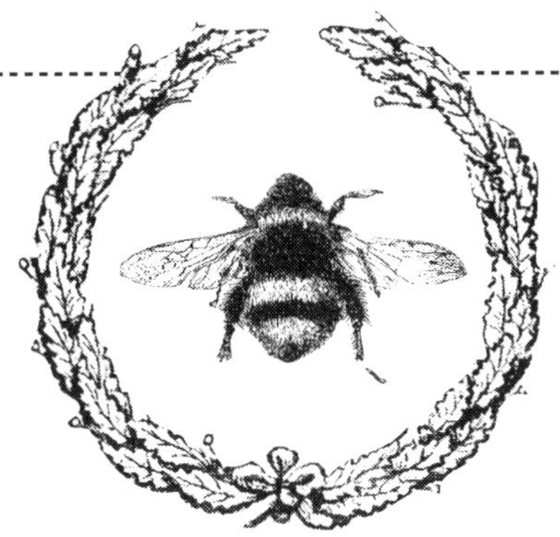

"Eat honey, my son, for it is good;
honey from the comb is sweet to your taste."

- Psalm 24:13, NIV

"'I will prevent pests from devouring your crops, and the vines in your fields will not drop their fruit before it is ripe,' says the LORD Almighty."

- Malachi 3:11, NIV

Lakes
& Streams

God has a purpose and plan for each of us:

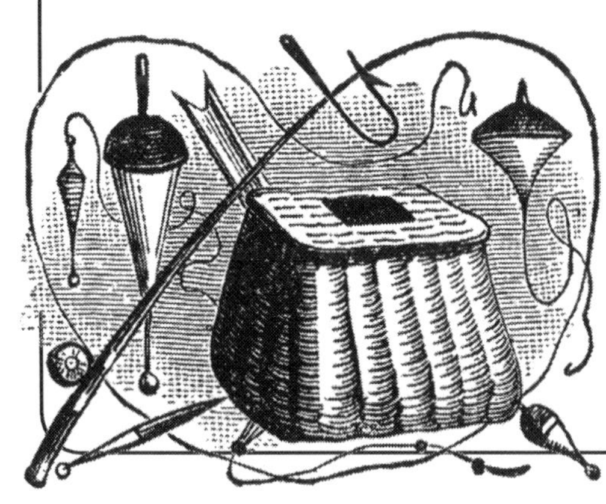

"'But now I will send for many fishermen,'
declares the LORD,
'and they will catch them.'"

- Jeremiah 16:16

Mentions of fish in the Bible:

Mark 6:41-42

Matthew 13:47-48

Luke 5:4-6

John 21:3

Matthew 17:27

And Jesus said to them, "Come... follow Me, and I will make you become fishers of men." Mark 1:17

What tools should one use to "fish for men?"

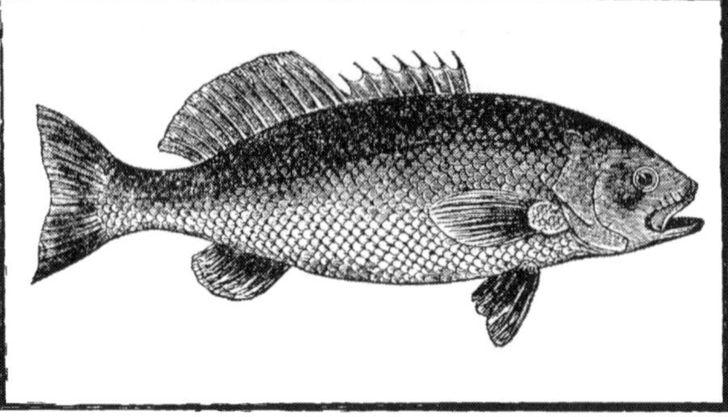

"The fear and dread of you will fall on all the beasts of the earth,
and on all the birds in the sky, on every creature that moves along the
ground, and on all the fish in the sea; they are given into your hands."

- Genesis 9:2, NIV

"Speak to the earth, and let it teach you; and let the fish of the sea declare to you. Who among all these does not know that the hand of the LORD has done this?"

- Job 12:8-9, NASB

Drawing Pond Life:

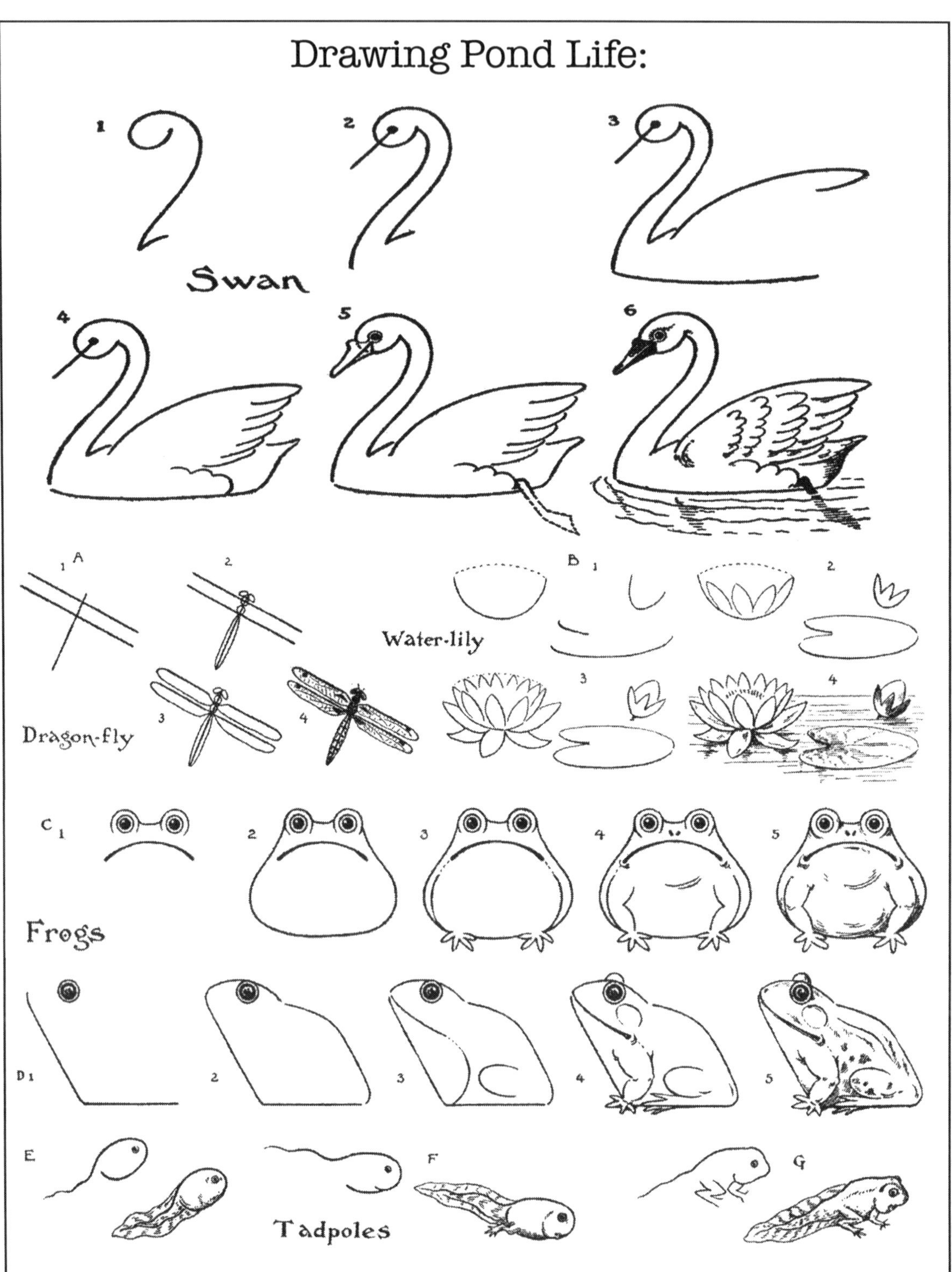

Now Put It All Together:

"I will make rivers flow on barren heights and springs within the valleys.
I will turn the desert into pools of water
and the parched ground into springs."

- Isaiah 41:18, NIV

"As Jesus walked beside the
Sea of Galilee, he saw Simon
and his brother Andrew casting a net
into the lake, for they were fishermen."

- Mark 1:16, NIV

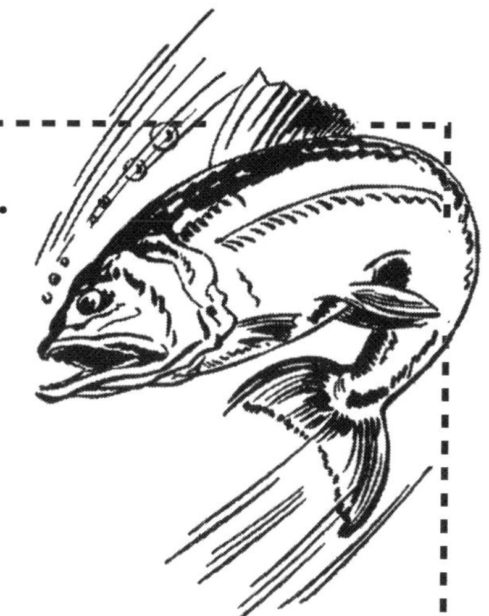

... and experiences we've shared.

"He blessed the food and broke the loaves and
He kept giving them to the disciples to set before them; and He divided
up the two fish among them all. They all ate and were satisfied."

- Mark 6:41-42

"Immediately, something like fish scales fell from Saul's eyes,
and he could see again."

- Acts 9:18, GWT

Rocks & Minerals

The Lord is my Rock

"The LORD is my rock, my fortress and my deliverer;
my God is my rock, in whom I take refuge,
my shield and the horn of my salvation, my stronghold."

- Psalm 18:2, NIV

The Rock of my Salvation

"Come, let us sing for joy to the LORD;
let us shout aloud to the Rock of our salvation."

- Psalm 95:1, NIV

Rubies
- Proverbs 31:10 -

Onyx
- Exodus 28:9 -

Crystals

Keshi Pearls

- Revelation 22:1 -

- Matthew 13:45-46 -

"But the LORD has become my fortress,
and my God the rock in whom I take refuge."

- Psalm 94:22, NIV

The stone that the builders rejected has now become the cornerstone.

- Psalm 118:22, NLT

"Let the words of my mouth and the meditation of my heart
be acceptable in Your sight, O LORD, my rock and my Redeemer."

- Psalm 19:14, NASB

"He lifted me out of the slimy pit, out of the mud and mire;
he set my feet on a rock and gave me a firm place to stand."

- Psalm 40:2, NIV

Three Kinds of Rocks:

Igneous

Metamorphic

Sedimentary

Rock of Ages

"They did not thirst when He led them through the deserts.
He made the water flow out of the rock for them;
He split the rock and the water gushed forth."

- Isaiah 48:21, NASB

A Firm Foundation

"…You shall stand there on the rock; and it will come about,
while My glory is passing by, that I will put you in the cleft of the rock
and cover you with My hand until I have passed by."

- Exodus 33:21-22

He Leadeth Me

"…upon this rock I will build My church;
and the gates of Hades will not overpower it."

- Matthew 16:18, NASB

Reptiles & Amphibians

Have you ever caught a lizard?

"The lizard you may
grasp with the hands,
yet it is in kings' palaces."

- Proverbs 30:28, NASB

How about a frog?

"Then frogs overran the land
and even invaded the king's bedrooms."

- Psalm 105:30, NLT

My thoughts on turtles:

"These also shall be unclean to you among the creeping things
that creep upon the earth; the weasel, and the mouse,
and the tortoise after his kind."

- Leviticus 11:29, KJV

My thoughts on toads:

NOTE: Have you ever wondered what is the difference between
a toad and a frog ? Both are tailless amphibians,
but frogs have smooth, moist skin, and toads have dry, warty skin.

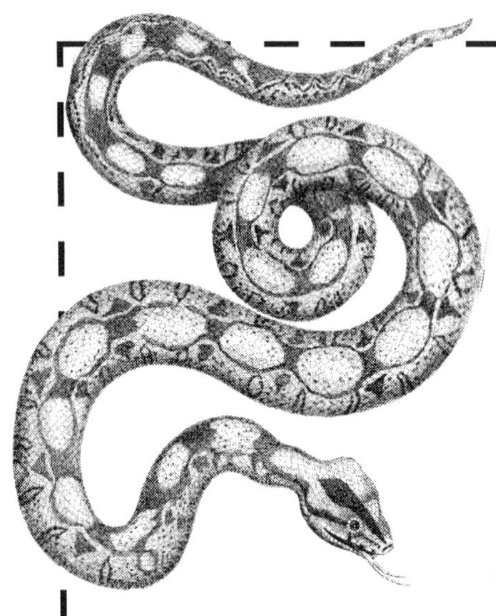

Look to Jesus and live.

"As Moses lifted up the serpent in the wilderness,
even so must the Son of Man be lifted up;
so that whoever believes will in Him have eternal life."

- John 3:14-15, NASB

Satan has already been defeated.

"He seized the dragon—that old serpent,
who is the devil, Satan—and bound him
in chains for a thousand years."

- Revelation 20:2, NLT

"The Nile will swarm with frogs,
which will come up and go into your house
and into your bedroom and on your bed..."

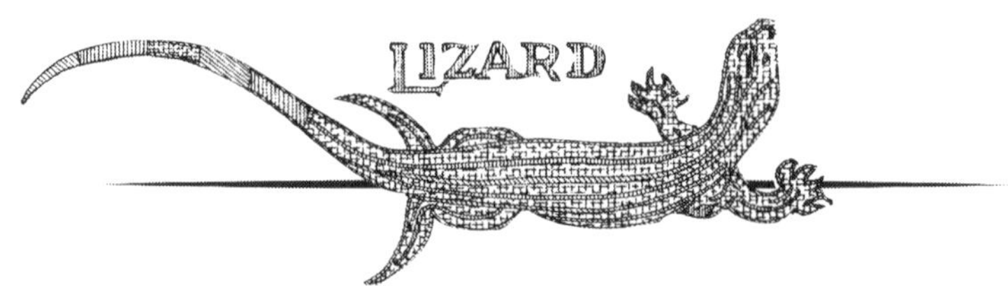

"...the gecko, the monitor lizard, the wall lizard,
the skink and the chameleon..."

- Leviticus 11:30, NIV

Annuals & Perennials

How do we encourage growth?

"Can papyrus grow tall
where there is no marsh?
Can reeds thrive without water?"

- Job 8:11, NIV

Growing Things:

Tools of the Trade:

"The blacksmith stands at his forge to make a sharp tool,
pounding and shaping it with all his might. His work makes him hungry
and weak. It makes him thirsty and faint."

- Isaiah 44:12, NLT

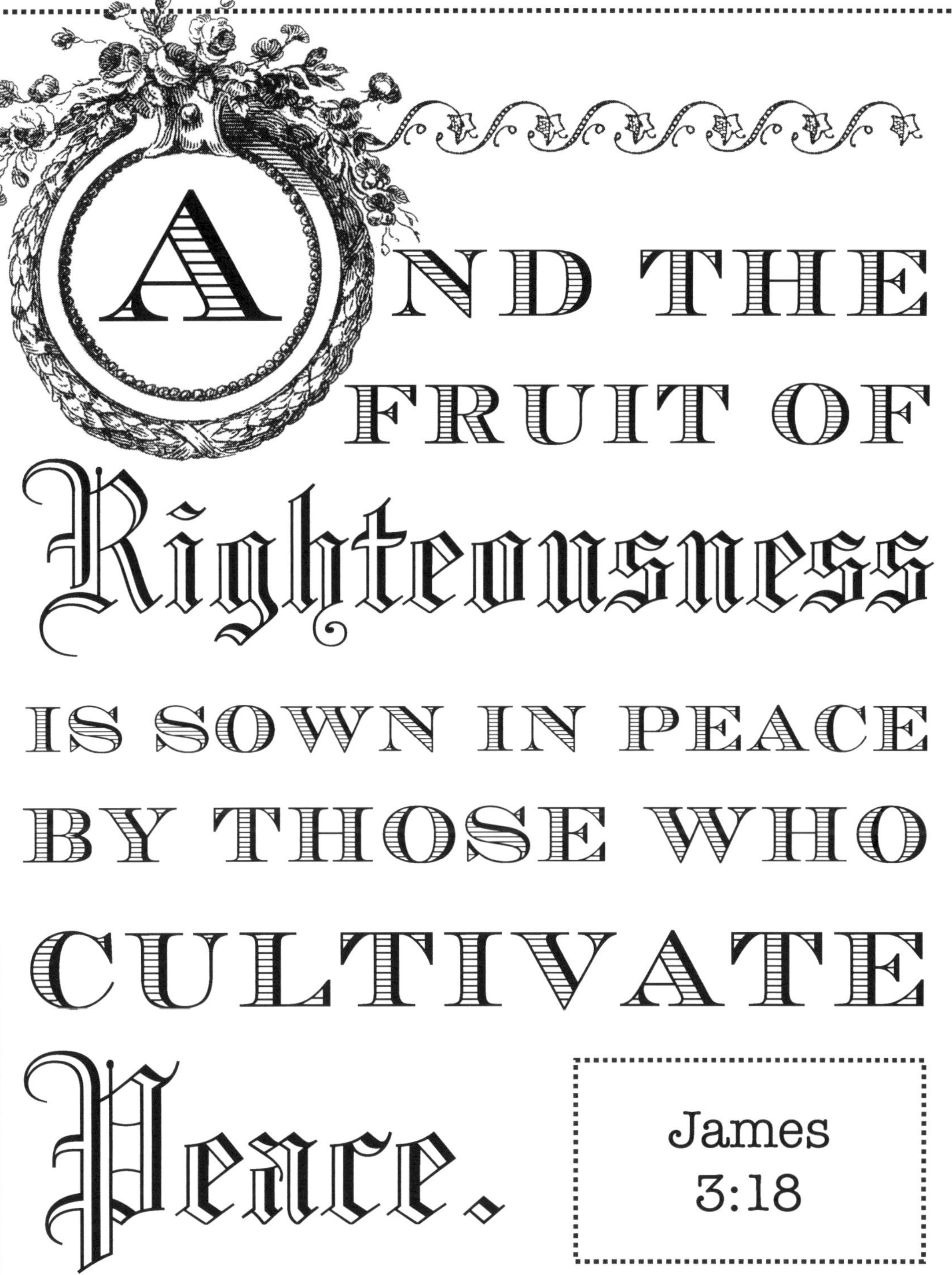
And the fruit of Righteousness is sown in peace by those who cultivate Peace.
James 3:18

How does your garden grow?

"I planted, Apollos watered, but God
was causing the growth. So then neither the one
who plants nor the one who waters is anything,
but God who causes the growth."

- 1 Corinthians 3:6-7, NASB

The Kingdom of Heaven
is like a tree in a garden...

"It is like a mustard seed, which a man took and planted in his garden.
It grew and became a tree, and the birds perched in its branches."

- Luke 13:19, NIV

"He cuts off every branch in me
that bears no fruit, while every branch
that does bear fruit he prunes
so that it will be even more fruitful."

- John 15:2, NIV

"On the vine were three branches. And as it was budding,
its blossoms came out, and its clusters produced ripe grapes."

- Genesis 40:10, NASB

"Before the mountains were born or you brought forth the whole world,
from everlasting to everlasting you are God."

- Psalm 90:2, NIV

Bulbs...

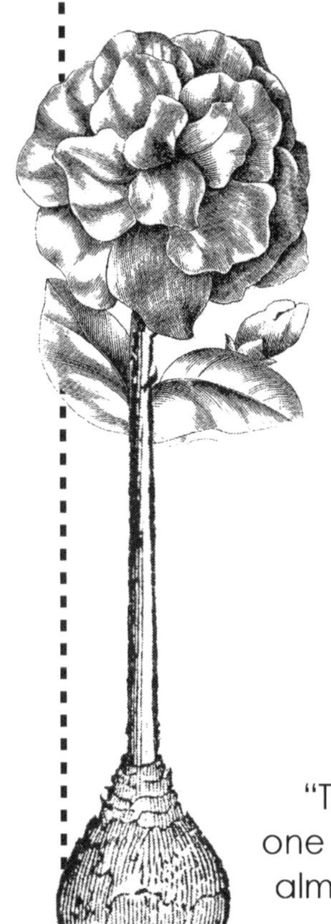

"Three cups shall be shaped like almond blossoms in the one branch, a bulb and a flower, and three cups shaped like almond blossoms in the other branch, a bulb and a flower."

- Exodus 25:34, NASB

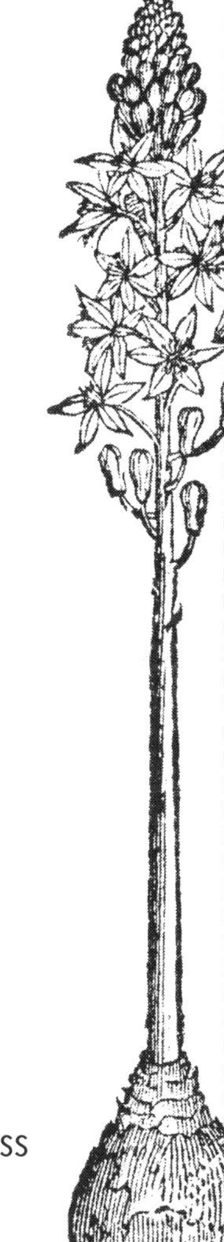

"The desert and the parched land will be glad; the wilderness will rejoice and blossom. Like the crocus, it will burst into bloom; it will rejoice greatly and shout for joy."

- Isaiah 35:1-2, NIV

Springtime Blossoms:

"Let us go early to the vineyards to see if the vines have budded,
if their blossoms have opened, and if the pomegranates are in bloom."

- Song of Solomon 7:12, NIV

"But the fruit of the Spirit is love, joy, peace, patience, kindness, goodness, faithfulness, gentleness, self-control; against such things there is no law."

- Galatians 5:22-23, NASB

"But the seed in the good soil, these are the ones
who have heard the word in an honest and good heart,
and hold it fast, and bear fruit with perseverance."

- Luke 8:15, NASB

Fall
Foliage

Fun Things to Do with Leaves:

"There is a time for everything,
and a season for every activity under the heavens..."

- Ecclesiastes 3:1, NIV

That person is like a tree planted by streams of water, which yields its fruit in season and whose leaf does not wither —whatever they do prospers.

- Psalm 1:3, NIV

"If you have faith as small as a mustard seed, you can say to this mulberry tree, 'Be uprooted and planted in the sea,' and it will obey you."

- Luke 17:6, NIV

"I will plant trees in the barren desert--
cedar, acacia, myrtle, olive, cypress,
fir, and pine."

- Isaiah 41:19, NLT

Leaf Shapes:

SAGITTATE
ACICULAR
LINEAR
OBLANCEOLATE
OBLONG
HASTATE
LYRATE
CORDATE
DELTOID
OVATE
ELLIPTIC
OBOVATE
OBCORDATE
ORBICULAR
RUNCINATE
OVAL
RENIFORM
LANCEOLATE

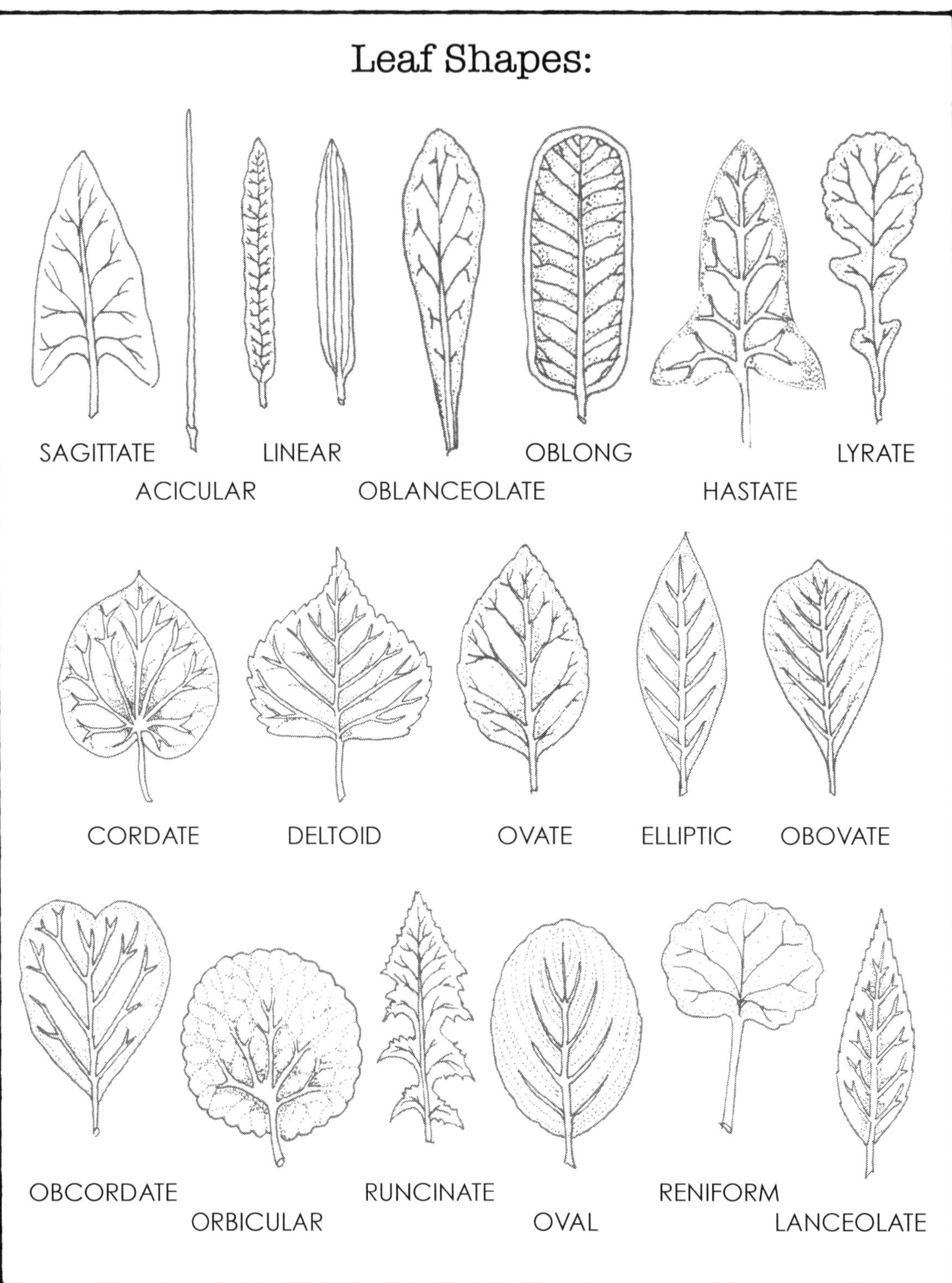

"He took one of the seedlings of the land
and put it in fertile soil.
He planted it like a willow by abundant water."

- Ezekiel 17:5, NIV

Why do trees drop their leaves?

"As long as the earth endures, seedtime and harvest,
cold and heat, summer and winter, day and night
will never cease."

- Genesis 8:22, NIV

Are there any "leaves" I need to drop during this season of my life?

"A lazy person doesn't plow in the proper season;
he looks for a harvest, but there is nothing."

- Proverbs 20:4, ISV

"Make a tree good and its fruit will be good,
or make a tree bad and its fruit will be bad,
for a tree is recognized by its fruit."

- Matthew 12:33, NIV

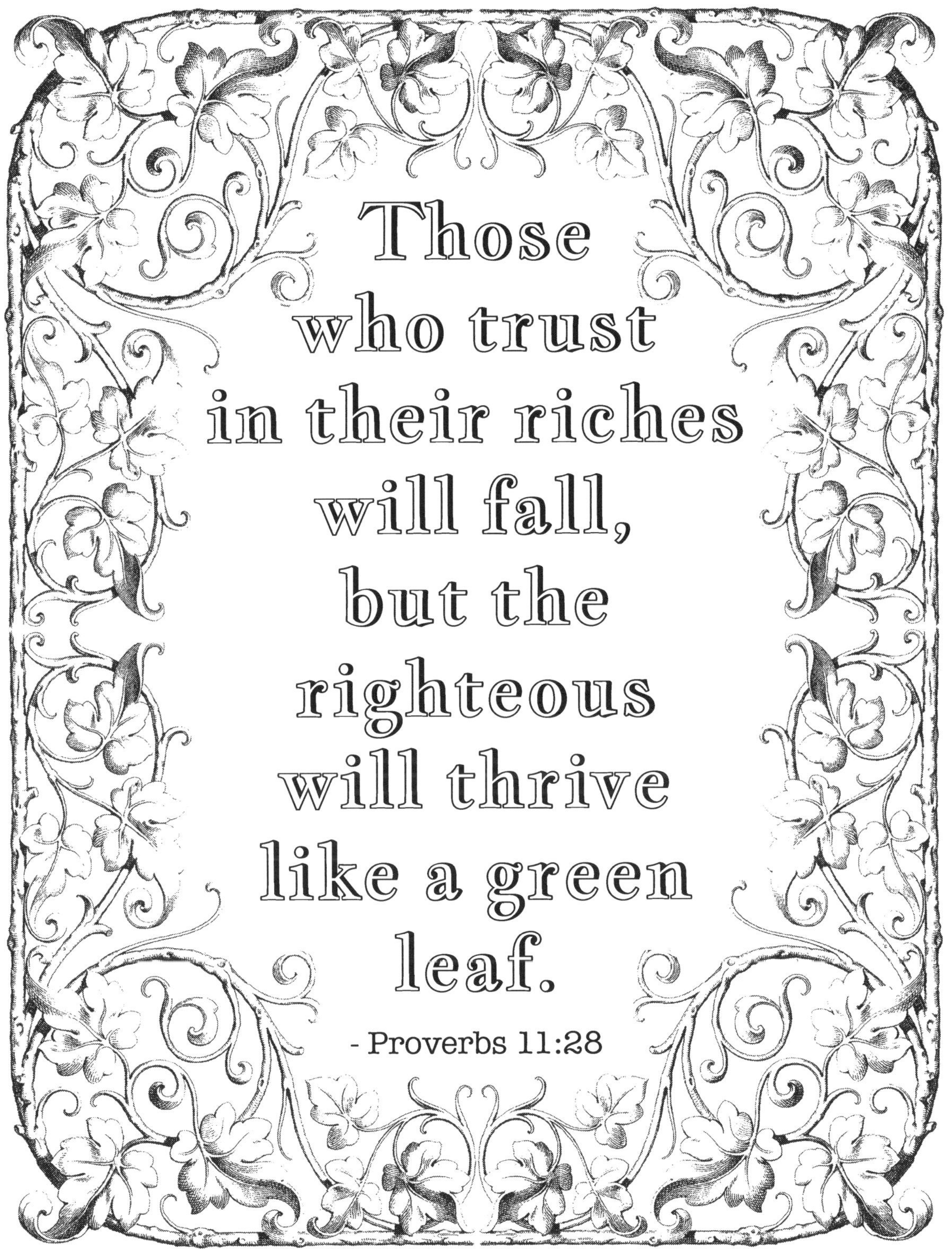

Those
who trust
in their riches
will fall,
but the
righteous
will thrive
like a green
leaf.

- Proverbs 11:28

"She considers a field and buys it;
with the fruit of her hands she plants a vineyard."

- Proverbs 31:16, ESV

Seashells & Seashores

"When it was time to leave, we left and continued on our way.
All of them, including wives and children, accompanied us out
of the city, and there on the beach we knelt to pray."

- Acts 21:5, NIV

… and the creatures we discovered there.

"So God created the great creatures of
the sea and every living thing with which
the water teems and that moves about in it,
according to their kinds….
And God saw that it was good."

- Genesis 1:21, NIV

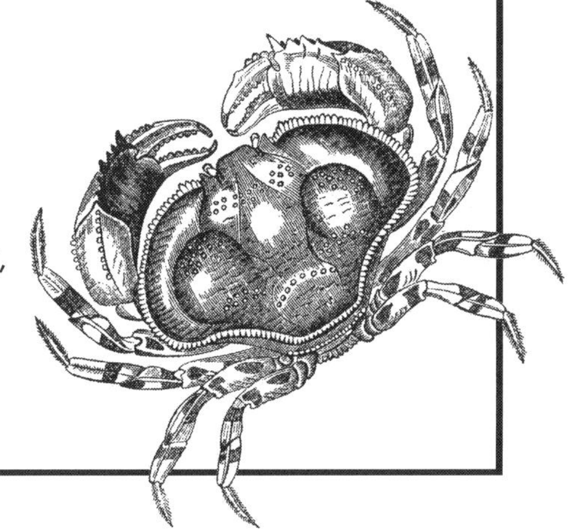

God's love for me is as vast as the ocean.

"There is the sea, vast and spacious,
teeming with creatures beyond number—
living things both large and small."

- Psalm 104:25

Even the winds and the waves obey Him.

"When Jesus woke up, he rebuked the wind
and said to the waves, 'Silence! Be still!' Suddenly the wind stopped,
and there was a great calm."

- Mark 4:39, NLT

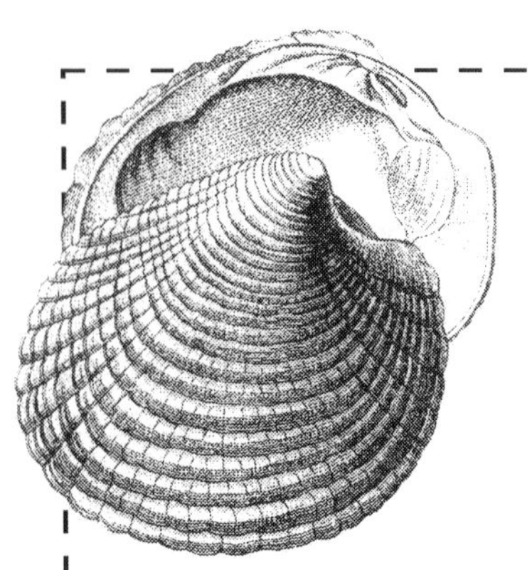

Collecting seashells...

... and building sand castles.

"But the person who hears and does not put my words
into practice is like a man who built a house on the
ground without a foundation. When the river burst
against that house, it collapsed immediately,
and was utterly destroyed!"

- Luke 6:49, NET

"Can you pull in Leviathan with a fishhook
or tie down its tongue with a rope?"

- Job 41:1, NIV

"I will sing unto the LORD, for he hath triumphed gloriously:
the horse and his rider hath he thrown into the sea."

- Exodus 15:1, KJV

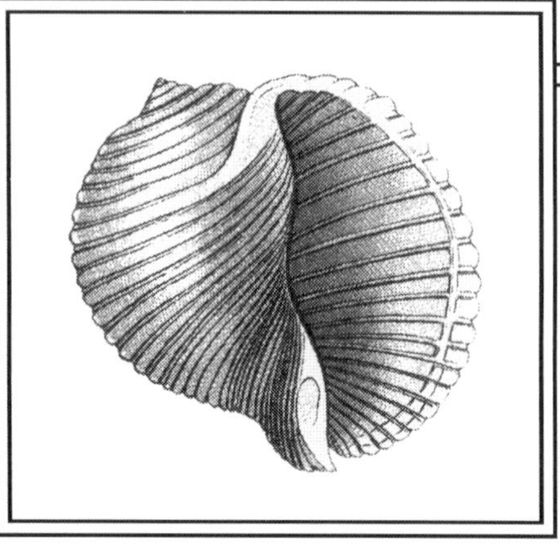

What gets me out of my shell?

"For God has not given us a spirit of timidity,
but of power and love and discipline.."

- 2 Timothy 1:7

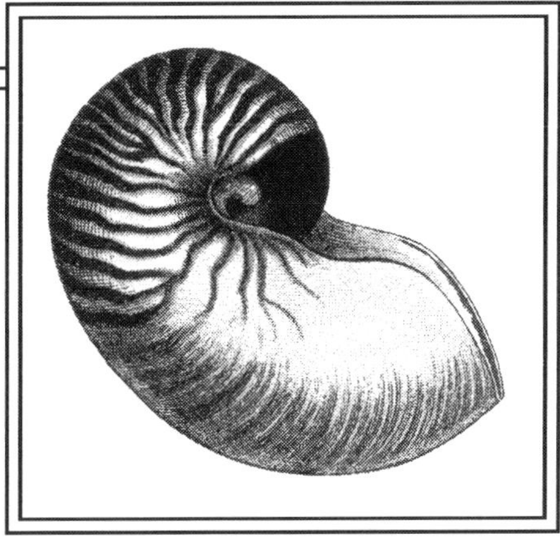

Home is where the heart is.

"For where your treasure is, there your heart will be also."

- Luke 12:34, NIV

I have decided to follow Jesus.

"When they had brought their boats to land,
they left everything and followed Him."

- Luke 5:11, NASB

Wherever He leads, I'll go.

"He makes me lie down in green pastures,
He leads me beside quiet waters."

- Psalm 23:2, NIV

Where can I go
from Your Spirit?

"…if I dwell in the remotest part of the sea, even there
Your hand will lead me, and Your right hand will lay hold of me."

- Psalm 139:9-10, NASB

Or where can I flee
from Your presence?

"And the LORD appointed a great fish to swallow Jonah,
and Jonah was in the stomach of the fish three days and three nights."

- Jonah 1:17, NASB

"When it was evening, the boat was in the middle of the sea....
Seeing them straining at the oars, for the wind was against them,
at about the fourth watch of the night He came to them,
walking on the sea."

- Mark 6:47-48, NASB

"We have this hope as an anchor for the soul,
firm and secure."

- Hebrews 6:19, NIV

"The seas have lifted up, LORD, the seas have lifted up their voice; the seas have lifted up their pounding waves. Mightier than the thunder of the great waters, mightier than the breakers of the sea—the LORD on high is mighty."

- Psalm 93:3-4, NIV

A Word from the Author:

I hope you've enjoyed working your way through this book as much as I enjoyed creating it. I've been making and keeping personal journals and sketchbooks—and lots and lots of scrapbooks—for over forty years. Doing this has brought me lots of pleasure, and I'm excited about passing on that love to other young people now through devotional journals like this one.

Additional volumes—something for every member of the family—are still in the works and will be released soon. If you have any questions or suggestions, feel free to contact me through my family's website, www.flandersfamily.info. Although I read every message I receive, time constraints do not allow me to respond personally to most of them. Those twelve children you see standing beside me in the photo at the top of this page keep me far too busy for that, at least in this season of my life.

If you have enjoyed this book, I would absolutely love it if you'd post a review saying as much on Amazon, Barnes & Noble, or Goodreads. Thanks so much. God bless and keep your thoughts centered on Him!

Also from Prescott Publishing

25 Ways to Communicate Respect to Your Husband
by Jennifer Flanders

25 Ways to Show Love to Your Wife
by Doug Flanders

100 Days of Blessing: Devotions for Wives and Mothers
by Nancy Campbell

Be ReVITALized: Moments with Michelle
by Michelle Kauenhofen

Get Up & Go:
Fun Ideas for Getting Fit as a Family
by Jennifer Flanders

Glad Tidings:
The First 25 Years of Flanders Family Christmas Letters
by Jennifer Flanders

How To Encourage Your Husband:
Ideas to Revitalize Your Marriage
by Nancy Campbell

How To Encourage Your Children:
Tools to Help You Raise Mighty Warriors for God
by Nancy Campbell

Life's Big Questions: Colossians
by Doug Flanders

Love Your Husband/ Love Yourself:
Embracing God's Purpose for Passion in Marriage
by Jennifer Flanders

The Prodigy Project (A Novel)
by Doug Flanders

More Books in This Series:

What Readers are Saying:

★★★★★ "My daughter adores the book! She loves that she can skip around and do what she feels like doing right then."

★★★★★ "Wonderful!"

★★★★★ "A fabulous book and I highly recommend it."

★★★★★ "I love how different each page is."

★★★★★ "As a teacher, I am thrilled that they are having fun mediating on His Word and practicing other skills i.e. reading, writing, and study skills."

★★★★★ "A great option for all ages."

★★★★★ "Fun, family friendly... exactly what I want my kids to ponder on — His Ways and the Truth."